African Wild Dogs

by Jane P. Gardner

Consultant:
Blaire Van Valkenburgh
Professor
UCLA Department of Ecology and Evolutionary Biology

BEARPORT
PUBLISHING

New York, New York

Credits

Cover and Title, © Nagel Photography/Shutterstock Images; 4–5, © De La Harpe, Roger/ Animals Animals; 6, © Red Line Editorial; 6–7, © BMJ/Shutterstock Images; 8, © Red Line Editorial; 8–9, © Ewan Chesser/Shutterstock Images; 10–11, © iStockphoto/Thinkstock; 12–13, © Animals Animals/SuperStock; 13, © Peter Betts/Shutterstock Images; 14, © Minden Pictures/SuperStock; 14–15, © Nick Biemans/Shutterstock Images; 16, © iStockphoto/Thinkstock; 16–17, © iStockphoto/Thinkstock; 18–19, © Minden Pictures/ SuperStock; 20–21, © iStockphoto/Thinkstock; 22T, © Hemera/Thinkstock; 22C, © Animals Animals/SuperStock; 22B, © iStockphoto/Thinkstock; 23T, © Ewan Chesser/ Shutterstock Images; 23C, © Peter Betts/Shutterstock Images; 23B, © Ablestock.com/ Getty Images/Thinkstock.

Publisher: Kenn Goin
Creative Director: Spencer Brinker
Photo Researcher: Arnold Ringstad
Design: Emily Love

Library of Congress Cataloging-in-Publication Data

Gardner, Jane P.
    African wild dogs / by Jane P. Gardner.
        p. cm. — (Wild canine pups)
    Includes bibliographical references and index.
    ISBN 978-1-61772-932-4 (library binding) — ISBN 1-61772-932-9 (library binding)
    1. African wild dog—Juvenile literature. I. Van Valkenburgh, Blaire. II. Title.
    QL737.C22G3727 2013
    599.77—dc23

                                    2013011507

For more information, write to Bearport Publishing Company, Inc., 45 West 21st Street, Suite 3B, New York, New York 10010. Printed in the United States of America.

10 9 8 7 6 5 4 3 2 1

❖ Contents ❖

Meet some pups

It is dawn and the sun is rising over the African **plains**.

Four African wild dog pups are already awake.

They are only a few weeks old.

Their older brothers and sisters are getting ready to hunt for food.

The young pups will stay home and drink their mother's milk.

African wild dog pups

What is an African wild dog?

African wild dogs belong to a group of animals called **canines**.

Pet dogs, foxes, and coyotes are also members of this group.

Adult African wild dog size

African wild dogs have large, round ears that help them hear well.

They also have long legs that help them run fast to catch **prey**.

round ears

long legs

Where do African wild dogs live?

African wild dogs live on plains in Africa.

These places are large, flat, and grassy.

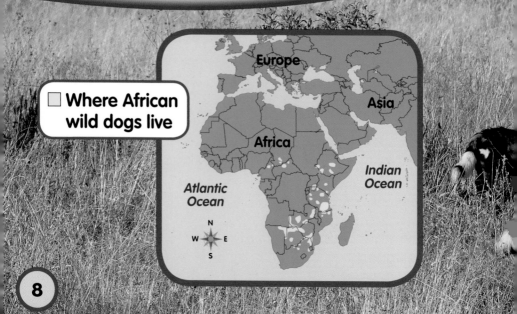

Where African wild dogs live

Europe

Asia

Africa

Indian Ocean

Atlantic Ocean

N
W E
S

The wide open spaces give the dogs lots of room to hunt.

African wild dogs do not live in one place for long, however.

Every few days, they move to a new spot to find food.

grassy plains

A wild pack

Pups live with their family members in a group called a **pack**.

A pack has between 5 and 20 dogs.

Each pack has a male and a female leader.

They are the pups' parents.

The other dogs in the pack are the pups' older sisters and brothers.

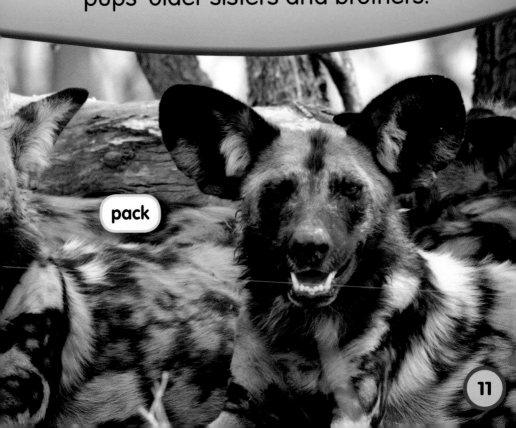

pack

A pup's life

A mother African wild dog gives birth to her pups in a **den**.

The newborn pups are born with their eyes closed.

However, when they are 13 days old, their eyes open.

a pup in a den

For the first month, the little dogs stay in their underground home.

During that time, the pack sleeps and hunts nearby.

The pack keeps the pups safe from **predators** such as lions.

lion

Time to eat

During the first ten weeks of their lives, pups drink milk from their mother's body.

When they are three weeks old, they begin eating meat, too.

pups drinking milk

The grown-up dogs in the pack work as a team to hunt prey.

They hunt near the den so they can quickly bring back food.

Colorful dogs

At first, African wild dog pups have fur that is only black and white.

When they are two months old, however, they start to grow brown or yellow patches.

pups

Their new fur helps them blend in with the tall grass on the plains.

This helps the dogs surprise their prey.

grown-up
dog

Out on the plains

As the pups grow stronger, they playfully bite and pounce on one another.

This helps them practice the skills they will need to catch prey.

When the pups are three months old, the pack leaves the den area.

The growing pups follow the pack across the plains.

Growing up

By the time an African wild dog is one year old, it is ready to hunt with the pack.

Male dogs stay with the pack all of their lives.

Female dogs leave when they are two years old.

They will join new packs where they will raise pups of their own!

grown-up
African
wild dog

Glossary

canines (KAY-nyenz)
members of the dog
family, including pet dogs,
wolves, and African wild
dogs

den (DEN)
a home where wild
animals can rest, hide from
enemies, and have babies

pack (PAK)
a group of African
wild dogs that live
and travel together

plains (PLAYNZ)
large areas of flat land

predators (PRED-uh-turz)
animals that hunt and
eat other animals

prey (PRAY)
animals that are
hunted and eaten by
other animals

Index

Read more

Gentle, Victor, and Janet Perry. *African Wild Dogs (Wild Dogs).* Milwaukee, WI: Gareth Stevens (2002).

Murdoch, J. D., and M. S. Becker. *The African Wild Dog (Library of Wolves and Wild Dogs).* New York: PowerKids Press (2002).

Learn more online

To learn more about African wild dogs, visit
www.bearportpublishing.com/WildCaninePups

About the author

Jane P. Gardner is a freelance science writer with a master's degree in geology. She worked as a science teacher for several years before becoming a science writer. She has written books about science, geography, history, and math.